Mastering QR Codes For Your MLM Business

Mastering QR Codes For Your MLM Business

Everything You Must Know Before Using QR Codes In Your MLM, Network Marketing Business!

Mike Driggers

Mastering QR Codes For Your MLM Business

Everything You Must Know Before Using QR Codes In Your MLM, Network Marketing Business

Copyright © 2011.

Printed in the United States of America

ISBN-13:978-1470055547
ISBN-10:1470055546

For more information, visit:

www.MLMQrCode.com
&
www.MikeDriggersBlog.com

LEGAL NOTICES

Acknowledgments

Many thanks and praises to GOD all mighty who has guided me on the path he has chosen for me.

This book is dedicated to my son Alex who is my driving spirit and my greatest accomplishment in life.

My Thanks go to my Mother and Father, who have always believed in me and have encouraged me to reach for the stars.

Special thanks go out to Gaby Aguilera who has been a tremendous support.

To all the great coaches in my life, whose teachings have had a profound impact on my personal and business life.

Table of Contents

What are QR Codes?

Even if you haven't directly heard about them, or know what they are, chances are that you've at least *seen* a QR code – even if you didn't realize it at the time.

QR or, "quick response," codes are most often compared to barcodes in explanation. And while they are very much like a barcode, in that they are a somewhat scrambled code that when scanned they have an actual meaning. They are also vastly different from barcodes.

Most simply put, QR codes are a way to connect offline activity with online activity. Every company in today's business environment has a website and their goal is to drive traffic to their website – QR codes can do that. These companies also want to entice new customers and place their brand foremost in the public eye. – QR codes can do that too. QR codes put a company's digital presence in the palm of the customer's hand, whether they're actually online at the time or not. They are a way to get your name out there and pass around your digital business card in a way like never before. QR codes can easily accomplish all of this and much more for your business. Considering all the benefits of QR codes, it is easy to see how they differ greatly for barcodes.

A QR code is a small, generally square code of black and white symbol. You can create these codes for free, and in a multitude of ways – all of which will be covered further on this report – in order to reach your customers. When a customer sees the QR code you've created, they can use their QR code reader (also to be covered later,) to scan the code with their iPhone, Android, or other smartphone equipped with a camera to view it. When they do, they'll be taken to a website or page that has been generated or linked specifically for that QR code. In addition to just linking customers to other websites, you can also set up a QR code to generate phone functions, activate email, IM, and SMS.

This has huge benefits to business, as you can now reach even more customers in ways like never before. And, when incorporated correctly, they can be a massive marketing tool that will both increase customer awareness of your company, and your profits too! Now you can call, text, and communicate with customers like never before!

One of the main reasons customers love QR codes these days, and why they're becoming such a hot topic among large and small businesses alike, is because they indicate that companies using them are on the cutting-edge of technology. By using a QR code, you're instantly telling a customer that you know how to take advantage of that technology, and how to use it to make it easier for them to shop with you; which in the end, is all any business owner wants anyway.

But even though QR codes may be viewed as something that comes with technological advancement, they've been in use since 1994. It was then that Denso Wave, a subsidiary of Toyota, used them along the line while manufacturing automobiles and automobile parts. Today, everyone has taken advantage of it and because Denso Wave has never patented them, they're considered to be open-source software.

As with most things techie-related, once something comes along it's not long before competition is close behind. Such is the case with QR codes. There are a few different types of code readers and code generator software programs, the most recognizable name among them being Microsoft's Tag Reader. While Tag Reader is similar to using QR codes, these have the downfall of only being viewable by one specific reader.

QR codes on the other hand, are open and available to everyone, no matter what kind of reader your customer chooses to use. Opting for QR codes in favor of any other kind immediately opens up your audience from a select few to an entire market.

But before we start diving into how to generate QR codes and how to use them for your small business marketing purposes, let's first look at some interesting stats on QR codes. With just a few of them, you'll see that like the smartphone itself, QR codes are not a new trend in technology, they're a new way of living.

QR Codes: Stats and Fun Facts

In case you are still not convinced that QR codes are the next 'big thing' in large and small business marketing, consider these impressive stats:

- Approximately 50% of people have seen, or at least know of, QR codes.

- Nearly 1/3 of people have scanned a QR code.

- 13 times as many people were scanning QR codes in December 2010 than in January 2010.

- Of all the QR codes scanned, 63% of them were scanned using an iPhone; 25% were scanned using an Android phone; and 12% were scanned using another operating system on a separate device.

- The android-using market share is expected to increase over the next 2 years as this software is associated with Google and therefore free to use, unlike Apple's OS that comes with the iPhone, iPod Touch, and the iPad.

- Even with these crushing stats, still only 6.2% of Internet users actively use QR codes. While that may sound discouraging, keep in mind that only 13% of Internet users are said to be Twitter users, and you can easily see how large of a number 6.2% really is.

- 33% of QR code users have an annual income of $50,000 or more.

- Those in the age group of 25 – 34 are twice more likely to use a QR code than people in any other age group.

So now that you're convinced that QR codes really are the next generation of marketing campaigns, and that they're going to be around for some time, you need to know how to create one, and what your customers will need in order to read one. The first is easy, but important. Don't be scared off by the idea of "working with codes" or being bogged down in techie-speak. Once you create your first QR code, you'll wonder what's been stopping you this whole time; and you'll soon be making a code for anything and everything new happening in your business.

You will need to be familiar with what your customers will require to read your QR code. This will enable you to better enhance their knowledge and skills on QR codes, which will drive more profit to your business. Even though the uses of QR codes are increasing in the business environment, there are still many individuals who are not knowledgeable about these codes or even what to do with them!

QR Code Readers

Even though there's not a lot of point in having a QR code reader if you don't even know how to create a code, it is important that you understand what a QR code reader is, because your customers will need one in order to access and benefit from your code. And, if you want to test out the code yourself or use QR codes in any other way than simply creating them, you'll also need to know what a QR code reader is, and how to get one. The good news is that getting a reader is even easier than creating a code!

A simple online search will bring up a list of QR code readers that can be downloaded and used to scan, read, and view QR codes. Like the software available for creating the codes in the first place, the software for scanning and viewing the codes is free – so there's no cost to your customers and they've got nothing to lose!

A popular QR code reader for the iPhone is i-nigma; in fact this reader is said to be the most popular code reader in the world! This may be because it can be used on any type of phone, as long as that phone is equipped with a camera. Android users can also use the app Barcode Scanner, which also works as a QR code reader.

With the rise of all the apps that allow you to scan checks and compare prices, also came the rise of the QR readers. Developers of these apps knew of the QR technology that was already highly in play and seized upon it, building in technology before consumers even knew they wanted it.

Generating QR Codes

Before you start trying to identify ways to use QR codes in your marketing campaigns to promote your business and help drive customers to your website, you need to know how to create one. More good news - Creating a QR code is free, and as easy as typing on your keyboard.

> **NOTE:** *Before getting your QR Codes created be sure to read the important message at the end of this chapter.*

Do a quick Google search for "QR code generator," and you'll come up with a full listing of websites that will allow you to create your own QR codes. Be warned that there are nearly as many websites offering QR code generators as there are codes themselves, and they all offer different things. While you'll be able to input simple text for your code on just about every site, others will let you create advanced codes that include things such as color, images, and your company's logo. So while it's easy to find a listing of websites that will allow you to generate your own QR codes, it's a little more difficult to find the right one for what you want to do with your code.

One example of a more "basic" type of QR code generator site is **beqrious.com**. Here you can create your own codes, and it's very easy. Input your text and you can choose to link that code to a website, a text number, a phone number, or an SMS (Short Message Service). You can also choose the size of your code, which will be important when we start considering using QR codes in different marketing practices later on. When you're just starting out making your own codes, these basic sites are generally a great place to start and will give you a real feel for what you can do with them.

An example of a QR code generator that is a bit more advanced and allows you to create more customized codes is **smartearl.com**. This website will let you choose a foreground and a background color, and will even allow you to choose your own error correction level, URL shortening, block size, margin size, output type and track your results. Once you get really comfortable using and creating QR codes in your marketing campaigns, the options can really be limitless on sites such as these!

Even these websites are just two of the hundreds, if not thousands, of websites that are out there allowing you to generate QR codes. So how do you pick the one that's going to be best for your business?

The first thing to always check is to ensure the code generator you're using is free. This is a no-brainer; with so many free offers out there, why pay for something when you don't have to?

The next thing to look for is how long it's going to take you to create a code. Even with the most complicated QR codes, it should take no longer than a few minutes. If it takes any longer than that, again there are simply too many other, faster, options out there to use anything else.

One of the factors that might not be so obvious, when you first land a QR code generating site, is whether or not it's safe and secure. You might be using your QR code to give out sensitive information, such as codes applicable only to some customers, or you might just be offering information or an e-book. Whatever you're using your code for, it should never have to go to a third party before the end user (the customer) is taken to the promised link or landing page. Keep in mind that it's your customers' email addresses, phone numbers, and IP addresses that you're playing with. If they fall into the wrong hands, such as a third party, they may be privy to privacy invasion and identity theft, among other things. In addition, if their information is up for grabs, yours probably is too just by using that generator website. So how can you tell?

With the exception of shortening links (which many generators do,) the user should never be redirected anywhere but the link you've put into your code. If they are, or if the generating website tells you they'll be redirected, find another website, software or provider to generate your QR code.

The last, not-so-obvious thing you want to look for in a QR code generator is whether or not you'll be able to measure its progress. While it might be a great marketing strategy to hand out business cards with QR codes on them at a workshop or promotion, you'll never have any way of knowing if people actually used them and if that marketing strategy worked. Make sure that analytics are available with your QR code, and you'll get so much more use out of them!

IMPORTANT

While there are many free options available to create your QR Code, it is critically important to know what you're getting yourself into. Not all code creation providers are created equal and some come with various fees and charges that are not expressed upfront.

Be sure to use someone you trust to give you all the information needed when making the best decision for you.

Designing Your QR Codes

While actually generating your QR codes is really a piece of cake, no website – no matter how advanced their codes – will be able to tell you exactly what to say with your QR code, or whether to direct them to a phone number, a URL address, or a text message number. Because of that, you'll need to determine those things before you even start thinking about generating codes. The actual look and destination of your QR code will play a huge part in the marketing practices you use them for, so it's best you become familiar with some basic QR code designs when designing your QR codes.

One of the biggest terms you need to be familiar with when designing your QR codes is "error correction." Error correction is essentially how much of the code will be automatically corrected when it's scanned or read. The higher amount of error correction in your code, the more you'll be able to add to it when it comes to things like images, logos, and artistic design. This is because the code is set up, through its error correction, to automatically correct and compensate for those things. So even though your logo isn't actually in code, it will still be able to be read and viewed – which is great for branding because people will not need to scan it to read it.

However there is a tradeoff. The higher amount of error correction you have within your QR code, the less storage capacity you have; so the less you'll be able to do with it and the less data you'll be able to put on it and give to your customers.

The four levels of error correction are:

- Level L – 7% of words within the code will be restored

- Level M – 15% of words within the code will be restored

- Level Q – 25% of words within the code will be restored

- Level H – 30% of words within the code will be restored

Just like operating systems, there are different versions of QR codes; but thankfully, there are not nearly as many versions of QR codes as there are operating systems. The *standard QR code* is what most people use to create theirs, and they usually have the ability to process and read larger codes. The standard character count for the standard QR code is 7089, although there are a few QR readers that can't read codes that large.

The *micro QR code* is a version of QR codes that are much smaller and are designed for readers that can't process larger codes. Although there are different versions within the category of micro QR codes, the maximum character count for micro codes is usually 35 numeric characters.

Of the three biggest things you need to know before creating QR codes, storage capacity is the third, but certainly not the least important. This of course, depends on the amount of information you'll be able to put within your QR code. The storage capacity of any QR code depends on the character count, the version of QR code software you're using, and the error correction level.

Customizing Your QR Codes

Now that you know some of the basics about designing your code, and you can even tell your customers how to use them, it's time to start really making your code stand out from the crowd. After all, we've proven that QR codes aren't going anywhere anytime soon. And as they become even more popular, you need to find a way to get yours noticed in a crowd of competitors. The good news is that it's super simple to do. All you need is your code, and your company's logo or an image you want to embed in the code.

The first thing you'll need to do is generate your code just as you want it. Embed your message, your URL, and anything else that you want to use to create your code, and choose the highest correction level there is. Remember that because you're embedding an image into it, you'll want to keep the rest of the message short; and you'll want to choose the highest error correction option there is.

After you've created your code through a QR generator, download it and import it to a photo editing program that supports layers; PhotoShop, GIMP, and Paint.net are all good options.

Once that's done, it's up to you to get creative and start playing around with your code and your image. For a simple layering job, place the image directly on top of the code.

Or, if you want to get a little more advanced, integrate your code right into and throughout the entire code – this is much more eye-catching and looks much more customized and advanced.

The last thing you need to do is test your code. Scan it with your QR code reader and see if you like the way it looks. If not, go back, play around with it, and make all the tweaks you need until you get it just right. It's so simple, and it really only does take a few minutes. What you'll get in return is the first step to a huge marketing campaign! And now that you're ready, with code in hand, let's start looking at how you can actually use QR codes, and how to create marketing campaigns designed around them to bring in more customers.

Maximizing your QR Code Marketing Campaigns

Okay, it's almost time to put the tech-speak away and get down to the fun stuff – how to *use* your QR codes in order to promote your business and of course, make more profit! But, before we get to all the really fun and creative stuff, there's still a little more work to do. This is the work that's involved with any marketing campaign and means understanding your demographics and the like. But because QR codes are relatively new to the public marketplace, and because many people are still unfamiliar with them, there are a few things unique to this type of marketing campaign than any other.

Understand your target audience:
With any marketing campaign, you need to know the average age, income, gender and geographic location of your target audience. But when talking about a QR code campaign, you also need to understand whether or not they need to be educated about QR codes, and explained how to use them. You also need to think about things such as whether or not your code requires a specific kind of reader; your customers will need to know this as well.

Know what your objectives are:

It's not going to do you any good if you send out a bunch of QR codes and don't really know what you want your company to get out of it. Be sure to have clearly defined goals before you start your campaign: do you want to grow your email list? Get more "likes" on Facebook? Promote your blog subscription?

Offer a value to your customer:

The QR code isn't going to do the customer any good if they don't get some value out of scanning and reading it. Because of that, you need to give the customer something in exchange for scanning the code. Some ideas are: 1) entering a contest for a chance for a prize 2) receiving a coupon 3) receiving a free ebook 4) speaking to a live customer service representative 5) going on a virtual tour 6) watching a product or service video or getting a free mp3.

Link your code to mobile-optimized sites:

QR codes are scanned by smartphones 90% of the time. The user will probably also use their phone to use the code and be redirected (to wherever you've sent them.) If it's a URL address, make sure the webpage is mobile-optimized, and not just mobile-friendly. The difference between the two is that 'friendly' means the page will be displayed relatively okay on a phone, while optimized means that the page is specifically designed for mobile users, and that it's actually best viewed on a smartphone.

Smaller images, solid colors:
There's only one reason for making these design elements as simple as possible. The less there is, the faster it will be for the customer to scan, download and view. The faster it is for the customer, the easier it is for the customer and the more likely they're going to use your QR codes.

Smaller links, smaller buttons:
This has nothing to do with download time, but instead will make it easier for the customer to touch and press these things when using your code. Ever tried to press a really, really small tab on a smartphone? It can be frustrating. Make sure that the customer will be able to access and use them easily and again, you've made your code instantly more convenient for your customer to use.

Test, test, and retest:
Your QR code isn't going to do anyone any good if it doesn't even work – and you need to make sure that it does! Test the code on the iPhone as well as on Android and BlackBerry platforms. You want to make sure your code is accessible to everyone – not just to users of one specific type of phone.

How to Use QR Codes

Let's identify some ideas on how to use your QR codes to provide appealing offers and discounts to your customers, or sign up new distributors? How exactly, to use them in order to bring appealing offers and discounts to your customers or to sign up new distributors? You can use these QR Codes to create labels for your brochures, products, cars, business cards, flyers, postcards, newspaper or magazine reviews, display banners and posters. There are so many things you can do with these QR Codes but don't worry if you're head isn't filling with ideas as you read; we've compiled a list of just a few places you can use QR Codes. After looking at the list, you'll no doubt develop a ton of ways you can use your QR Codes.

- **Create links to training.** Ensuring you team is thoroughly trained on the company, all products, and all techniques to build their Network Marking business is crucial to their success. You can provide them with a print out to access training from their phones during down times. You could also send them a PDF with various trainings to print or scan from the computer and download to their phones.

- **Promote team events.** In this industry events are the key to locking people into the company and the products. You build your business from event to event. You plan your goals and rank achievements from event to event. You motivate your folks to go to these events to stretch their vision on where the company is going and what is to come. You could put QR Codes on tear away post cards from staples and hand them to every team member. Promote the event, have nearest hotel locations, registration, schedules ect...

- **Create social networking cards** Create cards that you would hand out at your company major events to build your relationships and database of other distributors. These are different from your business cards. I would put my social media information on here like Facebook, Twitter, Youtube, LinkedIn, Google Plus, my blog or personal website and my phone number.

- **Link to a recruiting video** give out business cards, post cards or flyers with the QR Code to your companies recruiting video. You can buy tear a way cards from places like staples and print hundreds each day. Make sure to have your contact info and/or links to your site on there.

- **Motivational quotes or images** give out motivational quotes or images to your team, or potential customers/distributers on business cards, post cards or flyers.

- **Repetitive tasks.** Tired of having to explain how to get to a webinar or the number for the team call or the company call? Print a QR Code and tape it to their training manual or a business card they carry with them.

- **Create fun games for your team** Put In a jigsaw puzzle. This would create some real engagement as the user would have to put together the puzzle before scanning the image. The first person to get the message wins a prize. How about temporary tattoos that everyone wears each describing a part of the business or a product. The team has to go around scanning the tattoos filling in the blanks to questions you have asked. Whoever has the most right answers wins.

- **Offer coupons.** Customers love getting a discount – on just about anything! Wherever you put QR Codes, incorporate a coupon with them. Your customers will receive discounts just for scanning, and it will bring them into your business too!

- **Promote your opportunity event.** Lots of companies hold tons of events for many reasons. Link your QR Code directly to the online tickets to purchase; or an invitation to RSVP. How about on a flyer for the event with interactive maps like Google maps for where the event is.

- **Getting 'Likes' and 'Follows.'** Whether you're socially connected through Facebook, Twitter, or both, businesses are always looking to expand the number of people that are following them, because it's a direct indication of how many people are interacting, using, and involved with the company. QR Codes can take customers directly to your Facebook page or your Twitter profile; or you can even embed a 'Like" button right within the code – just by scanning it, customers will automatically 'Like' or 'Follow' you!

- **Increase your retail side.** Make sure to place QR Code's right on your products (if you can) or brochures so that your customer can easily use them to go straight to your product pages online to place an order or maybe repeat orders. This is also great if you're at an event or you just met someone and you don't have the product on you or in stock at that particular time of the sale. Your potential customers can scan the QR code and order it directly online (while standing next to you) and have them delivered straight to their door step. By doing this the potential customer does not miss out on your product, and you don't miss out on the new customer. Another great tip is to place different QR Codes with user reviews on or alongside the products. Your customers can scan the QR Code to see reviews of that particular product from previous customers. This is a great way to build credibility of the product and or brand.

- **Increase your email subscriber list.** Increasing the number of members on your subscriber list is another great way to get your name out there, promote your brand, and get new customers. Offer something enticing, such as special discounts or valuable and free information, that your customers will receive by signing up to your subscriber list. Then create a QR Code that will do it for them, or take them to a webpage where they can automatically sign up for the list.

- **Receive phone calls.** Create a QR Code that will make a phone call and again, give customers a great reason to make the call in the first place. Maybe it's a company overview, where they can listen to a recorded voice mail about the different products, product knowledge, company or testimonials.

  Maybe it's a direct line to technical support, or customer service (make sure to have your distributor ID on it as well). Whatever the reason, you've just put your customer directly in touch with you – and that's something every business wants!

- **Get customer feedback.** There's nothing more helpful to a business than finding out what its customers think about it, the services it offered, and the products available.

Incorporate a survey into your QR Code, or have the customer redirected to a website where they can participate in a survey and you'll instantly find out how customers think you're doing. This is great for getting testimonials Remember, offer an incentive for taking the survey; customers don't want to do something for nothing.

- **Scavenger hunts for your team and customers.** This is one of the main ways that people suggest using QR Codes. Compile a list of 3 or 4 codes that either have a physical location where customers can get specialty coupons, or a URL. Customers can collect the codes, visit the locations and get great offers. This is a fantastic way to get people out to new locations you want them to see.

Now that you know *how* to use QR Codes, the only thing left is deciding where to put them – and we have some ideas for that too!

Where to Place QR Codes

You've got the design down. And you know how to use your QR Codes in order to attract new customers, promote your business, and get new customers. The only thing left is deciding where to actually put your codes. After all, if your customers never see your codes, how useful are they going to be? Likely, they won't be helpful at all. In order to make sure that yours gets seen, here are just a few places to put your QR Codes:

- **Business cards.** This is probably the number one spot to put your QR Codes, and why not? How many business cards do you hand out in a day? 10? 20? 50? Increase your exposure by at least twice as much. – You will promote your brand through both the card and the code and your customer will be more likely to use you because there's a code attached to it. Rather than overload a business card with all of your contact info you could include the bare minimum for reaching you, then create a QR Code that leads people to your company replicated site, recruiting video, retail site, lead generation site or how about social media sites like: Twitter, Facebook, LinkedIn, YouTube, Flickr, Plaxo, Digg, Delicious, FourSquare, Stumble Upon, Yelp, and MySpace profile.

- **T-shirts Hats, and Buttons.** Put your QR Code on your t-shirt (or parka, in Maine, LOL), hat or buttons for some shameless self-promotion. A good example to make a bigger impression is printing 100 t-shirts and giving them out to people to wear. It could have a saying, your company logo or even the product with the QR Code. You could also teach your team members how to do this. They could wear them at major events or have them wear them in public or attend public event like a ballgames, street fair, and trade shows as a group. For more engagement from the crowd, put different messages on the shirts, so people take more scans of more of your codes. This will definitely create a buzz, and get people scanning your codes!

- **Stickers and magnets.** Put your QR Code On stickers to hand out. They link to a website where you change the message every day. It could be used as a place for resources. How about a site teaching and or educating your potential customers with tips and how-to's. Of course, you would have your company/ product information on the site with your contact information.

- **Product labels.** Imagine a patron takes home a bag of your wonderful product. They scan the QR Code on the label and are taken to your website where they can order more by the case and have it shipped right to their door. Plus, next time, they could get a discount just for using the code. You could also use the QR code for them to learn about your amazing opportunity and how easy it is to share it with others!

- **On your car window.** We don't want to think about the potential customers that walk by your car when you're out and about each and every day. Now at any time of the day your potential customers/recruits can learn about the product or opportunity– post a QR Code on your door or in your back window – could have a saying *"Shop Online for Discounts Scan the code below!"* They still get to shop while you're busy doing other things and you don't lose a customer or potential recruit!

- **On your laptop.** How often do you pull out your laptop at a coffee shop, on a plane, or on a train? Chances are a stranger or two has seen the outer casing of your computer and now's the time to turn that stranger into a customer! Slap a BIG QR Code sticker onto your laptop casing and when it is open anyone can scan it anytime, as long as you've got your laptop out (and you always do, don't you?)

[41]

- **Directly on your product.** We've talked about putting QR Codes on labels; this idea takes that one step further. Get really creative and find innovative ways to display QR Codes on your product. Sale cupcakes? Lay an edible QR Code across the top of super fluffy icing!

- **On trade show booths**. Create posters or flyers that you can hand out that would say something like "Scan the QR Code, (be entered to win) to receive a free sample.

- **As part of a personalized direct mail piece**. Each QR code can go to your replicated website or opportunity overview.

- **Newsletter or Classified ads, both online and offline**. Great way to create curiosity especially with a creative headline. Give some type of tips or sale your product or your opportunity.

- **Create a stamp**. Get stamp crazy and stamp everything in sight. Good example would be when you send any mail out (if you still pay bills through the mail, which I still do) stamp it and send a card with a QR Code on it. Also stamp the bill its self and the envelope.

Do you realize how many people will see it? It would be a different person each time. You could even stamp a post-it-note and hand write thank you with a marketing message like "Scan For A Free Sample" on it, then put the post-it-note on the bill.

- **Put It on Your Website or the Contact Us Page as well as all your Social Media sites.** People take a picture of your page on the screen and put your contact info in their contact list

- **Put it on your power point presentation** in the corner, buy the products or at the end of the presentation. This is great for giving access to product information, company websites or training materials that the user can download.

- **Create Table Tents.** When you host trainings or any sit down events create table tents that sit on the tables where your distributors and guest can scan them and get access to your training for the day, video of an event or maybe a thank you coupon for discount on the next event or product.

- **Name Tags.** When you have trainings, seminars, conferences or parties that require name tags create QR codes that have that person information on it or to a map or schedule for the days event.

- **Receipts or invoices.** How about a coupon for their next purchase on the bottom of the receipt. You could even promote the business to them from here. You could put, "Looking for part time to fulltime help scan this code for more information".

- **Lawn Signs.** These are signs that you see on the side of roads or at stop lights or even in front of people houses. You can promote your product and or opportunity from these signs. Put A large QR Code with a heading that says" Scan Here to find out more about this amazing ...."

- **Put it on the end of your marketing videos.** You should be creating reviews and overviews of your company product and opportunity. Creating videos promoting your opportunity or doing reviews of the opportunity and or product is a great way to expose the opportunity and or product. Put your contact information in the QR Code and place it at the end of the video or right after either the product description or opportunity description.

- **Put it on your luggage.** If your luggage ever gets lost...

Conclusion

Don't let the word 'code' scare you. QR codes don't involve any HTML, or knowing how the seedy underbelly of a motherboard works. While they are codes, QR codes are simply a way to connect your business' offline presence with its online presence – and in today's world, that's huge!

While there are a few technicalities to think about when it comes to the design and layout of your codes, we hope that we've been able to show you just how easy and fast it is to create QR codes. And, more importantly, we also hope that we've shown you how to use these codes to increase your business and get new customers. Because at the end of the day, that's all that QR codes are all about.

Next Steps

Thank you again for downloading this free report. We hope that you found it useful and it has given you the information you need to help you better understand the most important things you should know before using QR codes for your MLM –Network Marketing business.

If you would like additional assistance please contact us at:

Mike Driggers

408-890-7404
MLMQrCode@gmail.com

Recommended Resources

We know that dealing with QR codes can be very stressful. While we hope this guide has provided you with everything you need to we understand you may need further information and assistance. You can always contact us directly. In addition, we recommend these helpful resources as well.

Articles

http://www.MLMQrCodes.com/
http://www.5min.com/Video/How-to-Use-QR-Codes-268834323
http://www.abc15.com/dpp/money/consumer/data_doctor/how-to-use-and-create-qr-codes
http://www.fastcompany.com/1720193/13-creative-ways-to-use-qr-codes-for-marketing
http://notixtech.com/blog/21-qr-code-frequently-asked-questions
http://www.youtube.com/watch?v=fktYvYc75ck&feature=related

Free Code Generator

http://eepurl.com/hAQCY This is the FREE software that came with the ebook. If you have not registered yet please do so to get your activation key.

Free Online Code Generators

http://www.smartearl.com/ this has tracking capabilities
http://qrblaster.com/
http://beqrious.com/
http://www.qrdroid.com/generate
http://www.qreateandtrack.com/

Mobile App builder and QR Code

http://e68bfbpjyisclci-pl6-eflb77.hop.clickbank.net/

Customize QR Codes

http://www.youtube.com/watch?v=hvGfCJZEIpw

Denso Wave Homepage (Creator of QR Code Technology)
Make sure you check out Denso Wave for more information
on the technology.

http://www.denso-wave.com/en/index.html

www.ingramcontent.com/pod-product-compliance
Lightning Source LLC
Chambersburg PA
CBHW071648170526
45166CB00003B/1476